Just Hold My Hand

Second Edition

Written by Karen Franco

Illustrated by Gabrielle Taylor Jensen

Just Hold My Hand

Copyright © 2013 by Karen Franco

First Edition, February 2013
Second Edition, June 2016

ISBN-13: 978-0-692701-40-9
ISBN-10: 0692701400

Library of Congress PCN: 2016906919

All Rights Reserved. No parts of this book may be reproduced or utilized in any form or by any means, electronic or mechanical, including photocopying, scanning, recording, or by any information storage and retrieval system known or hereafter invented, without permission, in writing from the publisher.

To contact Karen Franco or to order a copy of this book, please visit www.karenfrancobooks.com.

Other books in this series:

Jacob's Hoop
What Makes Bella Special?

Published by
AMITY Publications
Barrington, NH 03825
www.amitypublications.com

Printed in the United States of America

Dedicated to...

My son, Jacob ... I love you.
K.F.

My inspiration, my brother, Brennan.
G.T.J.

Hi, I'm Jacob! I went to the fair today!

Sometimes it's hard for me to be in a crowd of people, especially when there are lots of loud noises...like when the big tractors start their engines.

When it gets too noisy, I start to feel uncomfortable. But Mom says, "It's okay. Just hold my hand."

That helps me when I'm scared.

I like to play all the games at the fair.

There are so many exciting choices. Sometimes I get frustrated and cry when I can't play them all.

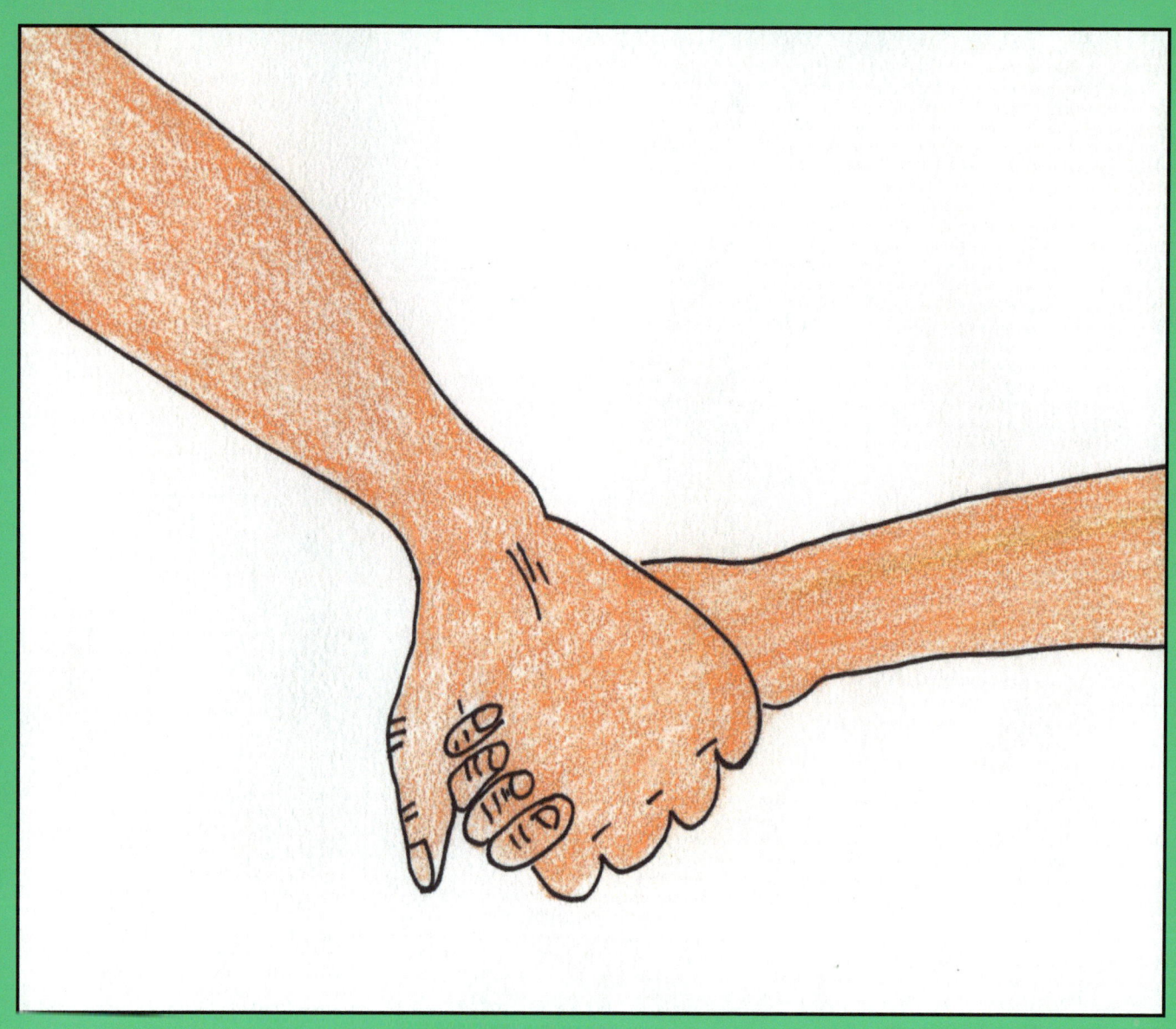

When I feel frustrated, Mom says,
"It's okay. Just hold my hand."

That helps me to feel better when I can't do all the things I want.

One of the games at the fair is to throw ping-pong balls into fish bowls.

I played and won two fish! I named one Mr. Fish and the other one Harry.

I wanted to play more but Mom wouldn't let me.
I got very upset.

Mom said,
"It's okay. Just hold my hand."

Holding her hand helps me when I need to calm down.

I watched a show where people trained dogs.

I yelled a lot during the show and that was bothering the dogs.

We had to leave and I felt bad.

Mom said,
"It's okay. Just hold my hand."

Holding Mom's hand helps when I need to remember to use my quiet voice.

I ate lunch at the fair. I like corndogs and popcorn.

I wanted to eat more and more but Mom said I couldn't.
I started to scream and cry.

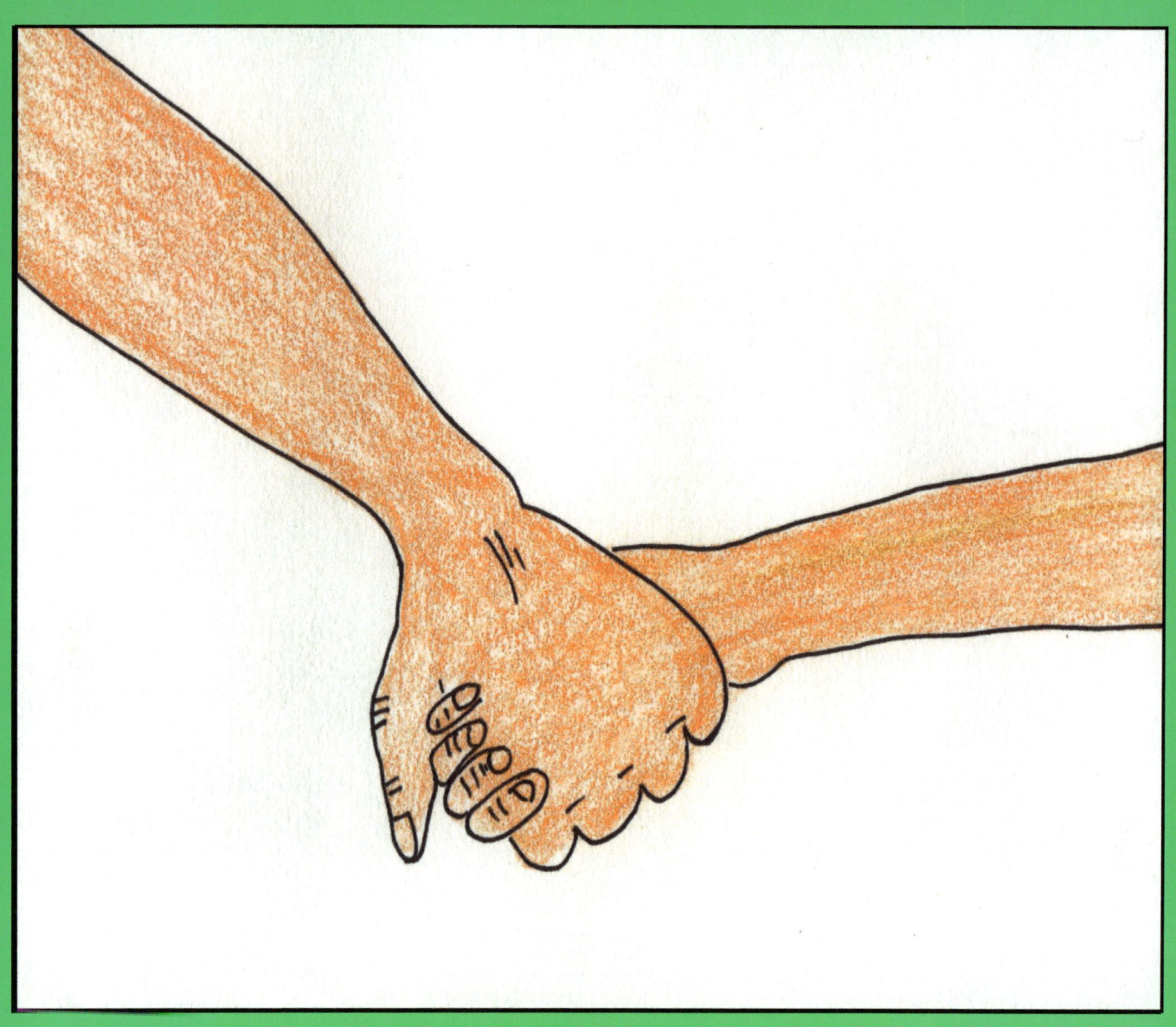

Mom said,
"It's okay. Just hold my hand."

That helps me to feel better when I can't get what I want.

I went on a hayride. When I sat down on the hay, it felt too prickly.

When I tried to stand up to get away from the itchy hay,
the driver had to stop the ride.

But Mom said,
"It's okay. Just hold my hand."

That helps me when something doesn't feel right
or if something hurts or bothers my skin.

I was excited when I saw the cows and the pigs.

I liked seeing all the farm animals but the air smelled funny.
I didn't like that.

Mom said,
"It's okay. Just hold my hand."

That helps me when I don't like something.

The day at the fair was over. It was time to go home.

It was a good day! I learned how to feel better when I get scared.
I learned how to calm down when I feel frustrated and upset.
I even learned sometimes things are different, just like me!

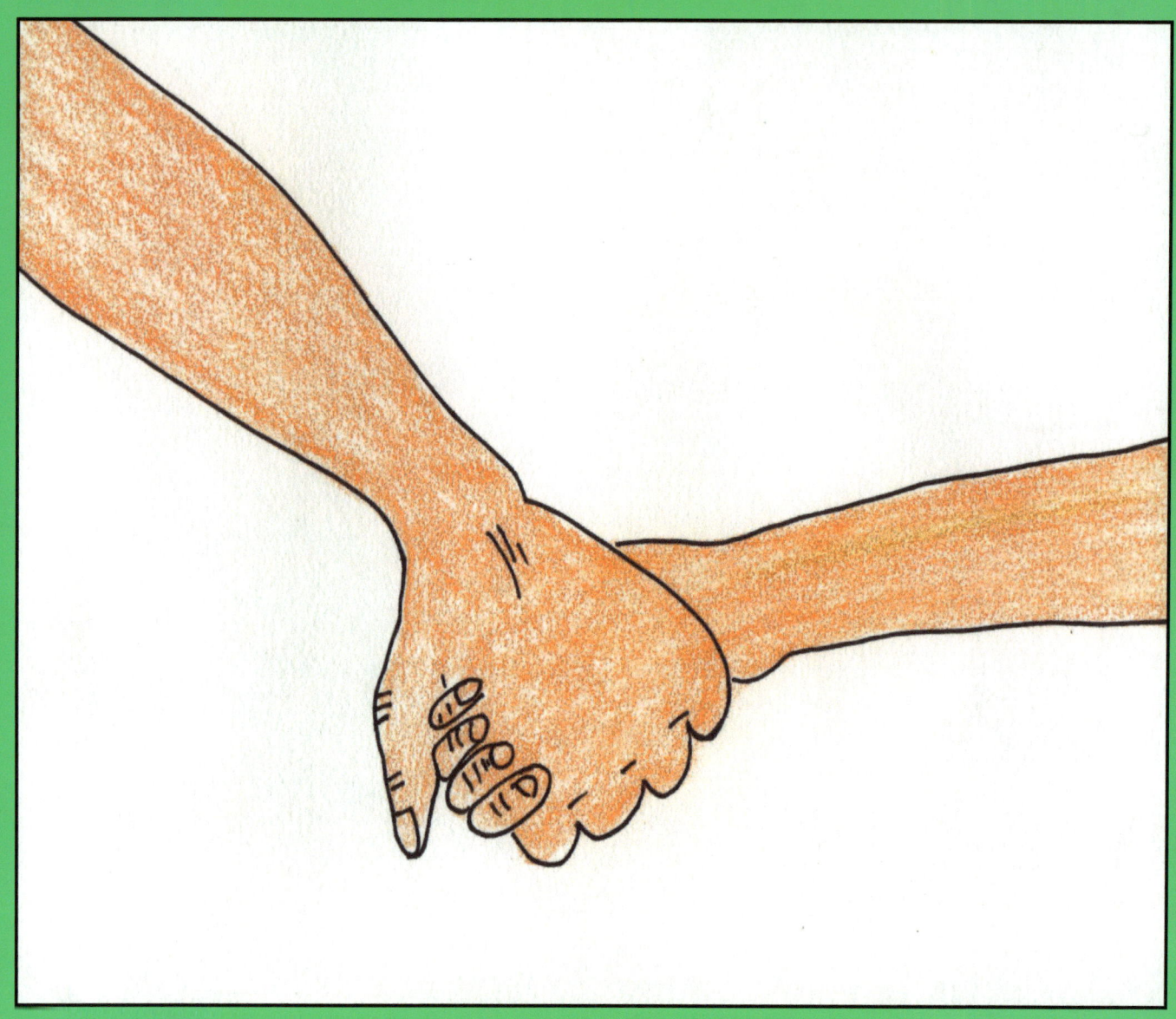

All of those feelings are okay! No matter what happens and no matter how I feel, Mom will be there to "just hold my hand."

Not the End ...

Meet Jacob

Jacob & Karen

Writing a book had never crossed my mind until after a few years of living in Jacob's world. It's quite an interesting place. My life has never been the same. Some days I feel like I'm a prop in a world that is truly Jacob's, where he feels safe, secure, and, I do believe, happy. Many years have gone by and I ask myself, "Where did that time go and how did we get to where we are today?" I have learned a great deal from Jacob. I knew having a child would be a rewarding and challenging experience but I never dreamed my life would consist of the day-to-day expectations that it does.

I didn't realize Jacob was different from other babies until he was one year old. I thought the developmental delays were because he was premature. When doctors and specialists talked about developmental milestones, I had no idea Jacob had his own agenda as far as development went. Jacob walked and eventually crawled, which wasn't his favorite thing to do, and the rest fell into place. Still, it took a lot of time for these developments to flourish. In fact, he didn't speak a word until he was five years old. Jacob became quite good at sign language and, for a child who couldn't speak, he somehow got his point across loud and clear. Now he doesn't stop talking!

Despite all the doctors we've seen and all the tests that have been performed, no one has been able to pinpoint Jacob's disabilities and how to help him. There are approximations and similarities to other disabilities but Jacob is unique in the fact that no one else has this particular deletion of the fourth chromosome. He has baffled the professionals. We've muddled through the medical world and have tried all sorts of treatments and therapies. Luckily we found a good mix of medications that helps Jacob function better in his day-to-day schedule.

It is my hope that sharing Jacob's journey may somehow help another family facing similar challenges and answer questions about how to cope, offer ways to help them see their child grow up and surprise everyone with what he or she accomplishes. When you realize you're not alone and that there are other people who are experiencing some of the same struggles with their own children, things seem a little easier. And, we will be the ones who are applauding the loudest at who our child becomes and what they accomplish.

Meet the Illustrator

Karen & Gabbie

Gabrielle Taylor Jensen is very much like every other eleven-year-old girl. She goes to school, works very hard, and gets good grades. She has friends and pursues her hobbies, such as horseback riding, animals, and art. She has had no formal artistic training, but she has an innate ability to create just about anything from cute cartoons to very serious dragons—and even magnificent horses. She was chosen by Karen Franco and Marybeth Zuhlke to work on this very book due to her aptitude with cartoon-style drawings.

Sometimes there is a higher power leading us in the right direction: When Gabbie was asked to do the artwork for the book, she said yes immediately. When asked what the book was about, Marybeth told her it was about a little boy named Jacob with developmental delays. Interestingly enough, Gabbie has two little brothers: Brennan, who is eight years old, and Bowen, who is five years old. Brennan happens to have Trisomy 21 which is also known as "Down Syndrome." This unique situation gives Gabbie the ability to put her heart into her drawings. She has a special gift that enables her to be able to read the facial features and body language that go with developmental delays in her brother. She realizes that even though Brennan can be challenging at times (as little brothers are meant to be), she loves him and always wants to be his hero—and so she dedicates this book to him.

Acknowledgment

I want to thank Marybeth Zuhlke for being such a positive influence on me. She helped me realize so many good things in life and what I can accomplish. She sent me "positive thoughts" along with wonderful quotes.

Two of my favorites were said by Eleanor Roosevelt . . .

~~~~~~~~~~~~

"You gain strength, courage and confidence by every experience in which you really stop to look fear in the face."

"You must do the thing you think you cannot do… "

~~~~~~~~~~~~

Everyone needs a little push to go after a dream.
Marybeth was my "push."

Thank you, Marybeth, for never letting me give up.

www.ingramcontent.com/pod-product-compliance
Lightning Source LLC
Chambersburg PA
CBHW041535040426
42446CB00002B/103